NAIL ART

NAIL ART

Inspiring designs by the world's leading technicians

Helena Biggs

ISBN 978-1-84858-976-6
AD002495EN

Manufactured in China

2 4 6 8 10 9 7 5 3 1

Contents

Introduction

In an era where individualism rather than conformism is largely celebrated, nail adornment is among the many expressions of creativity that have had the freedom to evolve. Particularly in the Western world, an explosion of colour and design in nail art has prevailed, with skilled technicians leading the revolution.

Nail colour has been present for more than 5000 years, originally in the form of 'lacquer' made from beeswax and flowers by the Chinese and henna used by the Egyptians to signify social order. However, it was only in the early 20th century that nail polish applied in various styles became part of a well-dressed woman's 'look'. Inspired by the high-gloss enamel used to paint cars, make-up artist Michelle Ménard adapted its use for nail colour in 1920, before collaborating with brothers Charles and Martin Revson and chemist Charles Lachman to create a hardwearing nail enamel in the years that followed. In 1932 they launched the first opaque nail colour, designed to prevent staining of the nail bed, under the brand name 'Revlon'. Hollywood stars and other pin-up girls led the trend for glossy red talons when MGM employed manicurist Beatrice Kaye to tend to the nails of the studio's actresses. She painted just the centre of the nails, introducing the half-moon manicure with the 'moon' of the nail left bare. The French manicure style also proved popular, designed to resemble the natural nail.

Arguably, the evolution of nail art stems from the French and half-moon manicures, which altered the one-colour form of the nail. With the launch of further colours, glue-on appliqués and fake nails for nail-biters, colour experimentation began and nail colour could be chosen to match lipstick shades. Trends in oval nails were prominent in the mid-1900s, largely as a result of influence from film stars and fashion icons, and the penchant for acrylic sculpted nail extensions began after the accidental invention of this use of acrylic by dentist Frederick Slack in 1957.

Below *Enjoying a relaxing manicure, Rosalind Russell in* The Women, *1939*

Fashion conscious Londoners in the Sixties used oil paints to decorate their nails with flowers, while the Seventies saw a craze for long, fake nails – expensive additions that were generally worn only by the affluent. The glue used was not water-resistant so longevity was poor, but the style led to the expansion of beauty salons as professional application became necessary. Jeff Pink of Orly produced the first French manicure kit, designed with nails to match all outfits in mind and make a French nail style easier to achieve. With increasing numbers of nail products and a growing global interest in nails, as well as growing numbers of trained professionals, nail competitions began, with technicians battling it out to produce perfect manicures.

In the Eighties and Nineties came the rise of image-conscious businesswomen who saw groomed nails as part of their professional appearance. This led to rapid growth in nail treatments and products and as expectations developed, so did the training and knowledge necessary to become a nail professional. The half-moon manicure made its way back into the spotlight with a modern twist, using a nail enamel shade to match an outfit with a contrasting colour to highlight the half-moon. Nail stickers evolved as an easy way to decorate coloured nails, and innovations in acrylic systems led to ventures with nail shape, such as stiletto, edged, squoval and even outrageous fantasy designs achieved through sculpting techniques.

French manicure styles remained popular with fashion houses, regarded as the style that suits all clothes, but nude shades were increasingly sported for this purpose. Outside this elite world, the nail technician, always considered as the afterthought behind hair and make-up artists, began to gain importance as groomed nails and their designs became pivotal to an overall look and growing health and safety awareness made it more desirable to visit a professional.

Above *A brightly coloured manicure by Leah Light using Minx nail foils.*

INTO THE 21ST CENTURY

Experimentation with materials, decals and additions to complement fashions grew more daring as nail technicians sought to create bespoke nails, and towards the turn of the century celebrity culture played a key role in further nail creativity. Super-manicurists carved their name in the fashion and editorial worlds with cutting-edge designs using unusual products, while hip-hop culture saw acrylic designs and sparkling talons make their way into the mainstream. Increasing numbers of women began to choose designed nails rather than the French style, showing that time, care and money had been spent on them.

While square French manicure acrylics, airbrushing effects and hooked, lengthy nails were not received well at first by fashion houses and businesswomen, the work of top technicians began to change their view. The nail art boom really hit in the early Noughties as a reaction to recessionary times. Technicians could tailor a service to suit all needs and budgets, so that what was once a luxury became a must-have accessory, and sales of nail polish reportedly increased from £68 million in 2005 to £152 million in 2012.

Nail colour and style are now increasingly accepted in many working environments as an often subtle nod to creative instincts, and with time-poor businesswomen and magazine photoshoots demanding speedy services, pre-adorned nails and the gel polish system have made their mark. Celebrity nails and further developments in nail art products, notably Minx nail foils, allow for instant nail effects and nail technicians are increasingly required to come up with imaginative, never-seen-before nails for both the consumer and fashion markets. Nail art has come to represent true artistry and skill, and the profession has seen its own set of rising talents.

Today, nail artists have become held in such esteem that their work warranted the first-ever nail exhibition, *Nailphilia*, in London in 2011. A successful US reality television show, *The Painted Nail*, based around a nail salon and its technicians, further highlighted the craft. A documentary, *Nailgasm*, explored nail art worldwide, while frequent innovations in nail products continue to fire the imaginations of nail artists all over the world. This book is designed to provide both instruction and inspiration for at-home creativity in a rapidly developing genre where art and craftsmanship are excitingly combined.

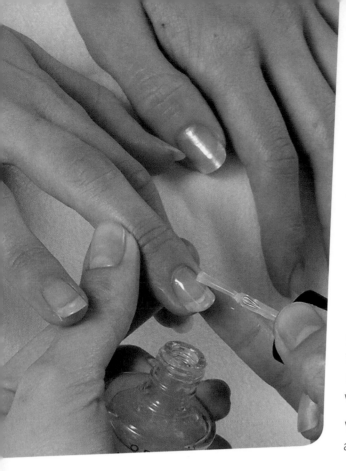

Getting Started

Before commencing the application of any nail product, it is important to prepare the nail. Good preparation maintains the health of the natural nail and ensures a smooth, shapely canvas on which to work. If preparation is skipped, nail products do not adhere well and can leave a poor nail finish, so even if professional nail technicians have little time on their hands, they will always perform basic nail prep.

A base coat is vital before any polish colour is applied to the nail as it prevents the nail from staining and contributes to the longevity of the design. As a general rule of thumb, apply a base coat in one thin layer to the natural nail and allow it to dry before applying a thin coat of colour. When this first coat of colour is tacky, or nearly dry, apply a second thin coat. Two thin coats dry faster and last longer than one thick coat of polish, which will simply peel off.

When a nail design is finished, apply a thin layer of top coat where possible and seal it at the edge of the nail to prevent chipping.

PREPARATION

Before you begin to decorate a nail, make sure that all the materials you need are to hand and you have enough time to complete your design.

Recommended Kit

- Base coat
- Buffer
- Cotton pads
- Cuticle pusher
- Hand sanitizer
- Nail file
- Nail polish remover
- Paper towels

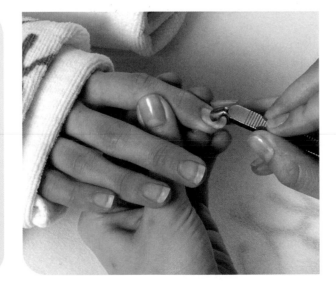

1 Tidy the cuticle area by pushing the cuticles away from the base and sidewalls of the nail, using a cuticle tool.

2 File the nails to shape. (For advice and guidance on nail shapes see p14).

NAIL GLOSSARY

Cuticle A layer of colourless, dead skin that clings to the nail plate and prevents bacteria from entering under living skin. Much of it is safely removed during a manicure.

Free edge The end of the nail that extends beyond the tip of the finger.

Nail bed The cells that support the nail plate.

Nail plate The main part of the nail. It appears to be in one piece but is constructed of layers, attached to the skin at the tip of the finger.

Sidewall The skin either side of the nail plate. The sidewalls act as a barrier against bacteria and viruses. The term also refers to the area of nail free of the nail bed, extending beyond the skin sidewalls.

Smile line The point on the nail where the nail bed ends and free edge starts. It is a half-circle that resembles a smile and can be artificially created by a nail professional.

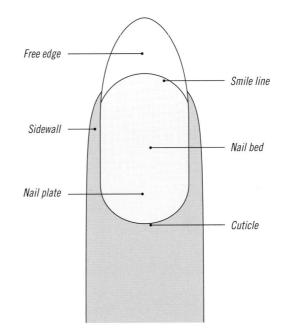

Free edge

Smile line

Sidewall

Nail bed

Nail plate

Cuticle

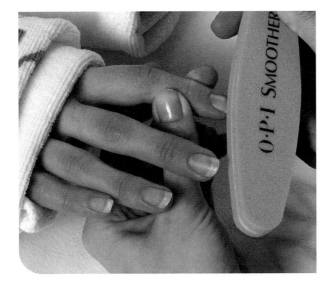

3 For a more pleasing finish, lightly buff the surface of the nail.

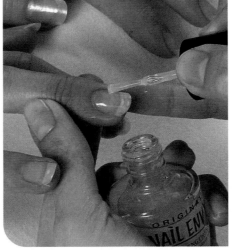

4 Apply a thin layer of base coat, leaving a 1mm gap around the edge of the nail, and wait to dry.

Top tip

If you have weak nails, use Nail Strengthener as a base coat.

CHAPTER ONE:

SCRATCHING THE SURFACE

Nail art in its most basic form can offer an effortlessly chic and stylish appeal, suited to a working environment or everyday wear. The classic French manicure – a pale nail with a white tip that enhances the natural nail colouring – has been subject to subtle changes since its inception, and the newer styles are suited to those who wish to make a statement with their nails without becoming too adventurous.

Variations on the classic smooth curve of the white tip include a polished or airbrushed chevron shape or a thick smile line, which is common if nails are fashioned by trained nail technicians using acrylic or gel with an artificial nail tip. These can achieve stunning results, provided you have a keen eye for colour, a steady hand and sufficient practice with nail products and tools.

The addition of glitter, gems and decals is popular for those who don't want to embark on outrageous artistry, and beautiful results can be achieved here with an incorporation of colour or a slight alteration in form.

Left *In an advertisement from 1951, Lisa Fonssagrives sports a full moon manicure, where the tip and base of the nail are painted in a contrasting colour to the middle of the nail.*

Tool Kit

What do you need?

1 A natural-looking nail shade in pale pink or peach to suit skin tone

2 A crisp or milky-white nail polish to create either a stark or natural-looking white nail tip

3 A glossy top coat for a high-shine nail finish

4 A base coat in a clear or pale shade

5 An artist's brush, such as Leighton Denny Precision Brush, to remove smudges of polish and style smooth design shapes

6 A statement shade to suit skin tone

7 Nail polish remover to take off existing polish and any smudges while you're working. You can also use it with a brush for design purposes

China Glaze Innocence   *CND Creamy Cameo*

China Glaze White on White

Orly Pointe Blanche

Leighton Denny Crystal Finish   *Orly Magnifique*

5

Artist's brush

4

Seche Base

Top five tips for nail polish application

1 Roll the polish bottle in your hands before application to give it an even consistency.

2 Hold back the skin on either side of the nail (the sidewalls) in order to reveal more of the nail area.

3 Apply polish in three strokes; in the middle, then the left of the nail, then the right.

4 Two thin coats of nail polish last longer than one thick layer.

5 Never flood the cuticle with nail polish. Always leave a 1mm gap around the nail to prevent peeling and give the illusion of longer nails.

6

Ciaté Power Dressing

Essie Raspberry

Leighton Denny Rebel

First stages of nail art

To achieve the best possible platform for nail art, a well-prepared nail is necessary. Preparation not only involves cleaning the nail area, but choosing the right nail shape to flatter both the fingers and the nail design. While nail design is often worn to make a statement, designs can be shown off best if they suit the wearer, so the chosen shades and nail shape are very important starting points.

Selecting the shape

Nails naturally vary in size and shape, from short fingers with short nail beds to long fingers with wide nail beds and every combination in between. The nail shape gives the foundation for a nail design and can complement the natural features of the hands. Nail technicians can use professional products such as gel or acrylic to extend and sculpt an artificial nail to the desired shape, whether it be a long, pointy stiletto style or a 'lipstick' nail – a shape with a slanted or angular edge.

The most common nail shapes are square, oval, squoval, round or pointed, achieved by filing. The choice may depend on lifestyle as well as aesthetics – although the options with short or bitten nails are limited.

1 The square nail is a popular choice for French manicures and can complement long nail beds and add length to fingers.

2 Oval nails offer a feminine look and can work with most nail beds.

3 A squoval nail is an extremely versatile shape, offering the length of a square nail with the soft edges of an oval.

4 Round nails are less noticeable and are popular with men as the shape mirrors the natural contours of the nail. A rounded shape can make large hands look thinner.

5 Pointed shapes are highly adventurous and not very common. However, they can create length and offer an artistic shape in themselves.

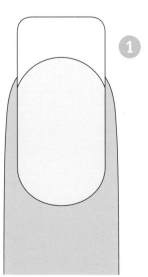

File straight up the sides and move across to the free edge to create.

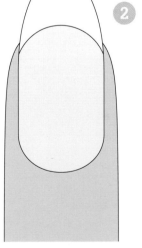

Use smooth, arching motions when filing to ensure a symmetrical finish.

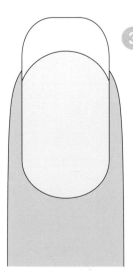

File the nail into a square shape then file underneath the corners to soften.

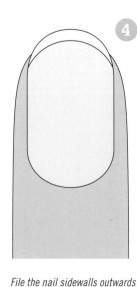

File the nail sidewalls outwards and round the edges into a curved shape to achieve the look.

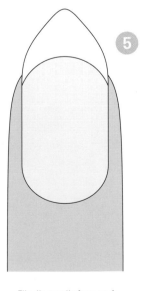

File diagonally from each sidewall to the middle point of the nail.

Choosing the colours

Following fashion and seasonal trends as a way of deciding upon a nail colour is fun, but professional nail artists are trained to choose shades that suit a skin tone in order to achieve the best possible finish. Just as with clothes, certain colours can be unflattering against the skin and even give it a ruddy appearance, while others can make it look radiant.

Shorter nails benefit from pale shades that give the illusion of length, with vertical stripes of nail art for a subtle finish. Those with longer nails can afford to be more experimental and draw attention to their nails with brighter shades and varied nail art.

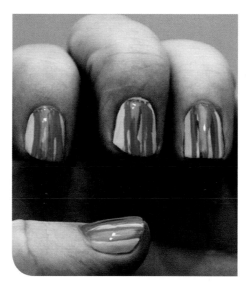

FAIR SKIN TONES

Most nail shades suit those with light or fair skin tones, although very pale skin may look sallow against extremely dark hues. Pinks, reds and lilacs work well to flatter fair skin.

MEDIUM SKIN TONES

Nail art can be carried off well by those with medium skin tones as varied prints and colours blend well with the skin. Metallic finishes and vibrant hues such as pink, orange, yellow or blue complement this tone; red, navy and dark purple should be avoided.

DARK SKIN TONES

Dark nail shades emphasize dark skin tones, and the warm hues of burgundy, red, green, gold and brown all look good. Tanned skin can also be complemented with lighter shades of blue and pink, but yellow-based colours are not recommended.

The French manicure

While the exact origin of the French manicure is unclear, it is believed that it was popular with fashionistas in Paris in the 1930s. Jeff Pink, founder of the Orly nail brand, stamped his mark on the style in the US in the mid-Seventies by branding one of his manicure kits as 'French' and it remains the most sought-after nail design worldwide. Its simple and classic style gives an effortlessly groomed appearance and nail technicians are often requested to craft it on the nails of models for photoshoots to coordinate with various clothing styles and suit a universal market.

Adopted by brides in particular, a French manicure can make a short nail look longer and slimmer if done properly and the style can be tailor-made to suit any skin tone by using variations on the classic pale pink shade. Common choices are peachy hues or even a clear polish to contrast with the white tip.

An accurate, steady hand is required when painting a French manicure tip. Stencils, kits and false nails with pre-painted tips can all make things easier, but applying a white tip with a polish brush can take some practice. Use a thin artist's brush to improve accuracy and keep the look understated by following the smile line – the line between the main area of the nail and the nail tip. Keep the white tip in proportion to the size of your nail bed; short nails look best with a thin white tip, longer nails can afford a thicker tip.

Below *Blue-tipped nails – a modern take on the classic French manicure*

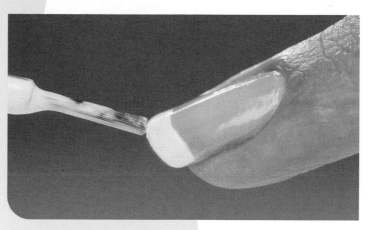

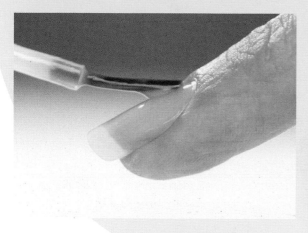

PROJECT: FRENCH MANICURE

1 Apply a base coat to the nail, not forgetting the underside of the free edge. While it is tacky, apply one coat of pale pink nail colour.

2 Paint a white tip using a smooth, confident motion and seal the free edge. Do not paint underneath the nail. Apply a second coat of white if desired.

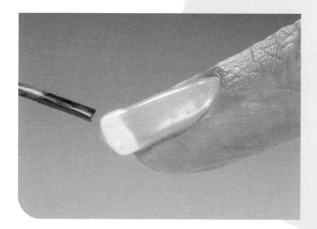

Top tip

Practise smooth, curved shapes with white polish on coloured paper before attempting the white tip on nails.

3 When the white tip is dry, sandwich it with a second coat of pale pink, painting under the nail and sealing the free edge.

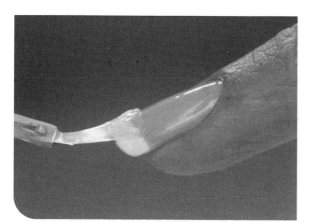

4 Lock in the manicure with a glossy top coat, again painting under the nail and sealing the free edge. Allow to dry.

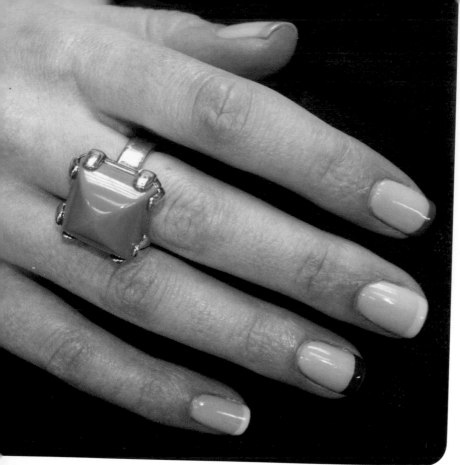

Variations on the French manicure

The French manicure has been subject to a number of variations over time, from the subtle to the bold and extravagant. A French style with the inclusion of nail art on the ring finger is popular with brides to signify the location of the wedding band. Whether it's a simple flick of glitter or a full, sculpted nail style, a slight addition to the French manicure can complement the detailing on a wedding dress without distracting from the dress itself.

The French style has also evolved with fashions. While it's still a staple nail design, technicians have experimented with tip colour for a subtle nod to a trend, or used a matte effect top coat on the majority of the nail before finishing with a glossy top coat on the tip.

Professionals can extend the nail tip and alter its shape to give the impression of elongated fingers. A long, white stiletto shape conveys grace and elegance and can incorporate glitters, 3D decals or sculpted additions for a more striking look. The tip shape can also be altered down towards the middle of the nail for a subtle appearance that channels chic high fashion; or perhaps there may be a thin line from the centre of the tip halfway down the nail or a jagged effect instead of a smooth smile line.

A 'reverse' French, or 'half-moon', manicure sees the colour or accent at the base of the nail, following the natural contours and colours of the nail itself. Other variations on a subtle, wearable trend include the 'halo' manicure, a thin ring of a contrasting colour around the edge of the nail in an oval shape.

Above *Nude French-style nails with multi-coloured tips by artists from Bio Sculpture Gel UK.*

Below *Candy-coloured French-style nails with dotted detailing, by artists from Bio Sculpture Gel UK.*

Above *A monochrome mix manicure in the French style with silver and diamanté detailing, by Megumi Mizuno.*

Left *An edgy variation on the half-moon manicure by artists from Bio Sculpture Gel UK.*

Below *A colourful half-moon manicure inspired by the sun breaking through a grey sky, by nail artists from Bio Sculpture Gel UK.*

TECHNICIAN PROFILE
Leighton Denny, UK

Leighton's passion for nails began when he watched his mother have a manicure while on a trip to the USA. Inspired by the creativity involved, he embarked on a career as a manicurist and went on to win a host of awards including Nail Technician of the Year for four years running. Leighton has a strong understanding of how to make hands and nails look healthy, groomed and beautiful and is famed for crafting chic and stylish designs. In order to appreciate every aspect of the industry, he began researching effective ingredients for hand and nail care and as a result he launched his own range of products, Leighton Denny Expert Nails.

Above *The French manicure with a pearlescent overlay.*

Main picture *A full-moon manicure in chrome nail shades.*

Moon manicures

Hollywood glamour girls in the late 1930s evolved the classic French manicure by leaving both the nail tip and the half-moon area at the base free of nail colour, a style coined the 'full-moon' manicure. A block of colour nail with a naked moon, or coloured half-moon, is a frequent style in advertising campaigns as it elongates the nail bed for a feminine look and epitomizes vintage-style charm.

After making a comeback in the 1990s, the style still holds great popularity, particularly with businesswomen who treat nails as an important part of their overall image. The half-moon has however been subject to experimentation in its evolutionary stages, with coloured half-moons and contrasting shades proving fashionable.

LEIGHTON DENNY SHOWS HOW TO CRAFT A HALF-MOON MANICURE

1 Apply the base coat but leave the half-moon area naked.

2 Apply two thin coats of your chosen nail shade (here Leighton uses Rebel from his own brand) and tidy the half-moon shape by using an artist's brush dipped in nail polish remover.

3 Apply a base coat to the half-moon and when it is dry, seal the colour with a thin application of top coat.

CHAPTER TWO:

COLOUR COMBINATIONS AND SPEEDY CREATIONS

Since the introduction of pigmented nail enamels by Revlon in the 1930s, cultural attitudes to colour have diversified. A willingness to experiment combined with social acceptance for several colours on the nail has seen colour clashes and simple, striking styles at the forefront of professional and at-home nail design.

Seasonal trends and fashion styles dictate nail colour collections, which in turn have a strong influence on the shades that are worn on the high street. Bright hues, neons and multi-colour combinations are universally popular in the summer months, followed by a tendency for warm reds, purples and glitters towards winter. The classic scarlet, made popular again in the 1940s by Hollywood actresses, is still a staple shade but subject to competition from 'nude' nails, which show chips less easily – ideal for busy women – and offer a plain canvas for occasional nail art additions.

The 1970s and 1980s saw the introduction of plastic fake nails to transform stubby natural nails into elongated and feminine shapes in a matter of minutes. Adopted by time-poor technicians and women in need of speedily groomed nails, fake nails have been subject to a design evolution, with artistic additions and ready-coloured surface layers. Stemming from the likes of nail stickers and decals that can quickly change a nail look, increasing numbers of innovative tools and instant effects polishes have made their way into the mainstream, encouraging further experimentation with colour and design.

Left *Adhesive 3D nail art designed and applied by Nazila Love Glamour.*

Tool Kit

What do you need?

1 A buffer to prepare the nail bed

2 False nails, with or without nail art additions

3 Nail glue or double-sided stickers for good adhesion of false nails

4 Nailtopia Floral Stickers

5 A nail-art placing tool for easy pick-up of small decals

6 Instant effects polishes and top coats in a variety of shades and finishes

7 Complementary shades for subtle nail designs

8 Base and top coat to prepare and seal nail designs

9 Statement shades and funky polish colours

10 A dotting tool for easy creation of spots with polish

11 Polish stripers or a striper brush for lines and outlines

12 A corrector pen or brush and nail polish remover to remove smudges

13 A sponge for a mottled nail art effect

14 Stencils and transfers for flat, expressive nail art with minimal effort

CND Girlfriend Buffer

Elegant Touch Pink Nail Glue

NSI Orangewood stick

Nubar Nail Gem Placing Tool

Top tip

An alternative to a nail-art placing tool is an orangewood stick or a pencil with a piece of Blu Tack on the end – ideal for picking up small gems and decals.

Elegant Touch Nails

Nazila Love Glamour Nail Glitz

Nailtopia Leopard Stickers

Nailtopia Florals

OPI Black Shatter

⑥

Essie Silver Bullions

China Glaze Crushed Candy Crackle Glaze

⑦

Cult Nails polishes in Let Me Fly and Manipulative

⑧

Lumos Top Coat

Lumos Base Coat

⑨

OPI Charged Up Cherry

OPI Need Sunglasses

⑫

⑩

Orly Instant Artist Dotter Duo

Art Club Striper in Pink Pastel

⑪

Nubar Hot Pumpkin 2-way Nail Art Pen

Essie Corrector Pen

Stick-on nails

Introduced as an economical response to the artificial nail craze of the 1980s, adhesive or 'stick-on' nail tips offer a quick fix for instant nail art. Ideal for short, unshapely or bitten nails, adhesive nails are favoured by session nail stylists who work on fashion shows or editorial photo shoots. To save time on set, they often pre-design the nails required for a photo shoot on plastic tips, then simply adhere and shape them to fit a model's nails.

French-style stick-on nails are common, as are clear or pink-tinted tips for a natural look. Nail art and polish can be applied on top of these tips and in recent years, tips manufactured with pre-applied nail art have entered the mainstream as a solution for those less attuned to freehand nail artistry. A vast range of shapes, colours and designs offer styles to suit any personality or theme and serve as an ideal outfit accessory, to be applied simply with adhesive stickers or nail glue.

Top left *Stick-on nails in embellished and tweed designs by Susanne Paschke of Supa Nails.*

Left *Hand-painted stick-on nails inspired by urban culture, by Susanne Paschke of Supa Nails.*

Right *3D press-on adhesive nails designed and produced by Nazila Love Glamour.*

Below *Tribal-style stick-on nails handmade by Susanne Paschke of Supa Nails.*

Five top tips for applying stick-on nails

1 Do not apply a base coat – simply buff the nail before application.

2 Use nail glue instead of stickers for longer-lasting nails.

3 Press the artificial nail firmly onto the natural nail and hold for a few seconds until secure.

4 To remove, gently lift the edge of the fake nail up and twist to the left and right until it loosens.

5 Avoid applying cuticle oil around the nail as this could weaken the adhesive.

Speedy art

Adhesive nails and pre-made designs have paved the way for loose decals and pre-made additions to create custom nail designs with little effort. Rhinestones, studs and small motifs add depth to a nail design and are easy to apply by placing them on a wet layer of top coat and allowing it to dry or by affixing them with nail glue. Trained nail technicians can increase the longevity of 3D items on the nail by setting them in nail gel or embedding them in an acrylic or gel nail extension. Those without a steady hand and skill for intricate design can lay nail stencils or transfers with words or patterns on top of nail colour before sealing with a top coat.

Products that provide instant effects on the nails with minimal effort can give the impression that a lengthy period of time has been spent on a nail design. Nails polished or crafted in a single shade can be turned into striking styles with glitter and crackle-effect top coats and metallic nail polishes, while matt top coats give a chic appearance. Matte black nails are popular with men, as are clear, matte treatment products worn to improve their nail health.

Magnetic nail products create an unusual and intriguing effect. Professionals use gel polishes for a longer-lasting magnetic look, but for a style that's simple to achieve without visiting a technician, consider nail polish that contains very fine magnetic metal particles. While the magnetic polish is wet, hover the magnet over the nail. This attracts the metal particles to the shape on the magnet and achieves an unusual but subtle effect.

Right Swarovski crystal-embellished toes by artists at Nail Systems International UK.

Left A bright nail design with two statement nails featuring decals and hand-painted dots, by Leah Light.

Below Nails in an assortment of bright shades with sparkly ring fingers, by Leah Light.

TECHNICIAN PROFILE
Leah Light, New Zealand

Leah has been working in the nail industry since 1995 and is internationally recognized as a highly qualified celebrity manicurist and senior nail educator. Her work was spotted by US celebrity gossip columnist Perez Hilton and Leah regularly contributes to his world-renowned website, providing insight into latest nail trends globally as well as nail art tips and tricks.

Above *Bright nails with assorted detailing inspired by modern artist Keith Haring and styled by Leah Light.*

Left *Nails styled to replicate a woman's blouse and featuring gold studs.*

Left *Freehand skulls painted in white over a black nail shade.*

Below *Neon pink nails with a statement shoe design handpainted on the third fingernail.*

PROJECT: THE STATEMENT NAIL By Leah Light

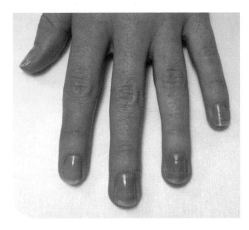

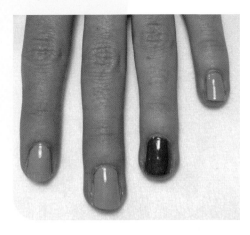

1 After preparation, apply a base coat to the nails.

2 Paint a thin layer of the chosen statement shade on the ring-finger nail and apply one coat of a contrasting or complementary shade on the remaining nails.

3 Apply a second coat of each colour to give full, even coverage. When dry, apply a top coat and cap the free edge.

The finished look; turquoise nails with a contrasting shade on the ring finger and gold embellishment.

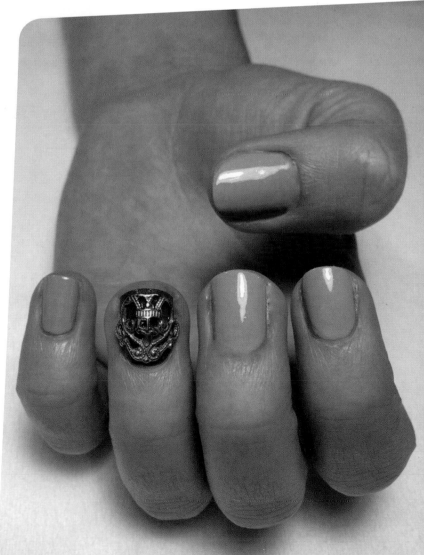

4 Add another layer of top coat to the ring finger and while it is still wet, place an embellishment on the nail and hold until the polish is dry.

Shade and product suggestions

Cult Nails polish in Manipulative
Cult Nails polish in Let Me Fly on the ring finger
Nail Veil embellishment from Chronicle Stones

Dots vs stripes

Dotted designs are simple to achieve with the right nail tool, and their versatility makes them a popular choice with professional technicians. Whether randomly placed or in a structured pattern, large or small, in one colour or several, a few dots can instantly transform a plain manicure.

Above *Monochrome nails with varying sizes of dots and stripes, by Megumi Mizuno.*

Below *Bright pink and purple nail styling with black outlines and detailing crafted with a striper, by Leah Light.*

Precisely circular shapes are difficult to achieve with a standard nail brush because of its width and the sparsity of the hairs, but a nail-dotting tool can give the appearance that a stencil or transfer has been used. By simply cleaning the tool with a wipe and nail polish remover, you can easily change polish shades to create a multi-coloured effect. If you're aiming for a more random effect, use stripers or the polish brush to create dots of differing sizes and shapes.

Stripes require a steady hand and a calm working environment, but once you have mastered the technique you'll be able to create a wide range of designs. Stripers or nail art brushes dipped in nail polish and slicked across a painted nail is an effective look. You can begin to build a more advanced nail design using varied thicknesses and colours, and experimenting with the direction of the stripes will give an even more striking appearance.

You can use striping tools to outline shapes and sections of the nail as a guide for applying different shades. Combine dots with stripes and vary styles and shades across the nails for a bespoke look.

Right *Nails with an assortment of stripes, dots and the half-moon style by Leah Light.*

Below *Deep purple nails with statement dots and stripes, by Leah Light.*

Top tip

Ensure that dots and stripes are thoroughly dry before adding a top coat or the colour may run.

Colour combinations

The range of colour combinations is as vast as your creative imagination could wish for, with virtually every shade on the colour spectrum now available in polish format. Chosen to suit personality, mood, outfit or occasion, nail art can feature clashing colours, muted shades or monochromes. An 'ombre manicure' is a subtle and popular nail finish where each nail is painted in a varying tone of the same colour, dark on the thumb then gradually getting lighter towards the little finger.

Colour experimentation allows for flat nail art that is powerful and striking and is suited to those who struggle with intricate designs and artistry. Multi-coloured nails suit the adventurous or those who find it hard to decide which overall shade to choose, and the contrasting shades can be varied each season and with each manicure.

Below *A purple ombre manicure using Bio Sculpture Gel. The effect is achieved by using varying shades of a chosen colour across the nails, from a light to a dark hue.*

Above *A neon and nude nail colour combination with Minx nail foil detailing, by Leah Light.*

Right *Three contrasting shades are used in this geometric style by Leah Light.*

Below *A dazzling colour combination with magenta shapes and silver chrome detailing, by Leah Light.*

Right *A striking chevron nail design in neon yellow, nude and black by Leah Light.*

Below *Colour-fade nails in contrasting shades of nude and black, by Leah Light.*

Below right *Jade nails with random black and silver overlays and shapes, by Leah Light.*

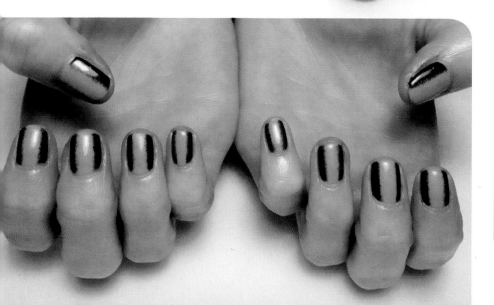

PROJECT: MULTI-TONE NAILS By Carly Eva

Nail technician Carly Eva uses OPI polishes to create a quick and colourful design on nails, using a sponge for a mottled polish finish.

1 First, apply a base colour of nail polish in two thin layers.

2 Apply three chosen shades to a sponge.

Top tip

Use white as a base colour to make bold neon shades appear brighter

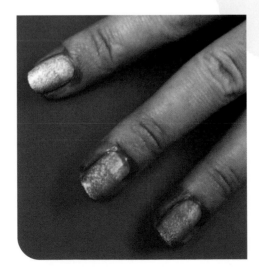

3 Press the sponge against the nail and rock from left to right for full nail coverage.

4 Reapply the polish to the sponge and repeat for an intense look.

Striking neon multi-tone nails created using a sponging effect over a white base colour.

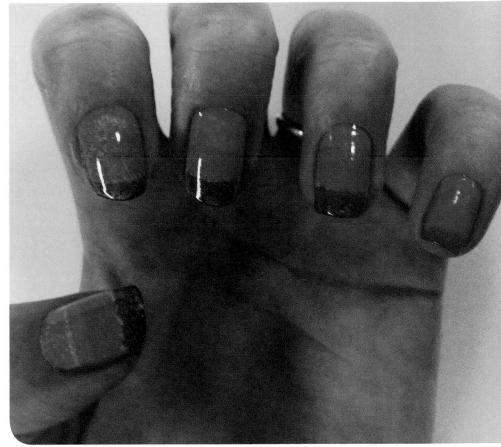

Shade suggestions

OPI Nail Lacquer in White Base
OPI Nail Lacquer in Formidably Orange
OPI Nail Lacquer in Riotously Pink
OPI Nail Lacquer in Seriously Purple

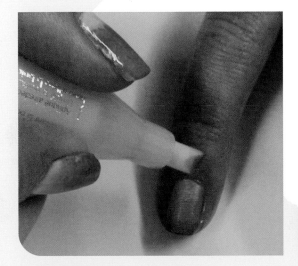

5 Remove excess polish with a corrector pen.

6 Apply a top coat to seal the design.

CHAPTER THREE:

NAIL ART FROM THE UNDERGROUND

City eccentricity and a penchant for pushing boundaries has led to an explosion of Pop Art-inspired looks and bright, funky statement nails. Hand-painted designs are taken one step further as intricacy and colour take precedence to really make nails pop, and a ghetto-glamorous theme runs through to create eye-catching works of art.

While the style was originally popular with cult fashion collectives, professional nail artists have made outré designs more acceptable to the mainstream media by drip-feeding wacky and colourful designs into consumer magazines where the nails take the spotlight.

Anything goes when it comes to underground artistry – nails are styled however the mood or the outfit dictates, and neon colours with decals or illustrations and slogans are often prominent. This style can afford to be a little rough around the edges; not all nails have to match and the beauty is in the knowledge that designs are hand-drawn with a striper or thin brush.

Left *An edgy freehand blue and white design hand painted on extended almond nails by Ami Vega.*

Tool Kit:
Nail art from the underground

OPI Alpine Snow

Models Own Black Magic

CND Asphalt

What will you need?

1 Black, grey and white nail polishes – staple base colours for urban-style nail art

2 Nail polishes in a variety of bright hues

3 Nail art stripers or a striper brush to use with polish, and a dotting tool

4 A strong top coat to maintain designs

Orly Green Apple

Essie Bright Tights

Zoya Pippa

Top tip

Find inspiration from fabrics, street art and trends. Print pictures and create mood boards to refer to while working on nails.

Right *An assortment of bright, freehand nail designs in contrasting colours, including tribal patterns, sea shells and leopard print. By Sophie Harris-Greenslade.*

Orly Instant Artist in Hot Pink

Orly Instant Artist Striper Brush

Nubar Basic White Striper

3

Nubar Black 2-way Nail Art Pen

Orly Instant Artist Large Dotter

4

China Glaze No-Chip Top Coat

TECHNICIAN PROFILE

Sophie Harris-Greenslade, UK

After graduating from university with a degree in illustration and animation, Sophie Harris-Greenslade completed a nail technician course and took up nail art full time. Her artistic talent means that she paints each nail design with incredible detail and precision and she has worked at London Fashion Week, on high-profile editorial shoots and with a number of celebrities. Sophie's blog, *The Illustrated Nail*, has a following of over 120,000 worldwide, placing her at the forefront of London's bespoke nail scene. Sophie has also teamed up with the Nails Inc brand to create a new nail art menu.

Above *Mismatched urban-style nails in blue, nude and orange with black detailing.*

Left *Bright yellow nails with a hand-painted lace effect.*

Far left *Intricate African-style freehand-painted designs on long almond nails.*

Left *Horse and floral thumbnail designs in monochrome shades.*

Right *A striking tribal-style nail look.*

Below *Jet-black nails with gold embellishments in a halo manicure style.*

Sophie's top five tips for creating street-style nail art

1 Practise designs with a nail art pen on paper before you start work on the nail.

2 Stay calm and relaxed throughout.

3 Steady your working arm on an armrest or with your other arm.

4 Seek inspiration everywhere, from television to fashion and nature.

5 Black and white polishes are great as a canvas. Keep two of each in case one bottle runs out or is broken.

Above *Stripes, spots and geometric shapes in contrasting shades are used to create a tribal design.*

Below left *Summertime-themed freehand-painted designs in a number of shades, including an anchor, lips, palm tree and personalised nail.*

Below centre *Extended nails inspired by flames are embellished with red gems for a 3D effect.*

Below right *Extended almond nails with a sparkly monochrome fade outlined in black.*

Left *Bright orange nails with a freehand white seashell and coral design outlined in black.*

Bottom right *A kaleidoscope design created by painting varying sizes of triangle shapes in four complementary shades.*

Below left *A mixture of bright nail designs suited to summer, with inspiration sought from cherries, tattoos and tribal patterns.*

PROJECT: NEON LEOPARD-PRINT NAILS By Sophie Harris-Greenslade

Fun, quirky and surprisingly easy to create, multi-coloured leopard-print nails are a popular twist on the classic print. The key to this striking design is contrasting, bright colours and a random pattern. Colour placement can be sporadic, and the black outlines of the spots should be of differing length for a realistic spotting effect.

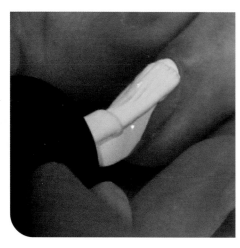

1 Apply one coat of white nail polish to all the nails.

2 Apply a second coat of white to the nails and cap the free edge. Allow to dry.

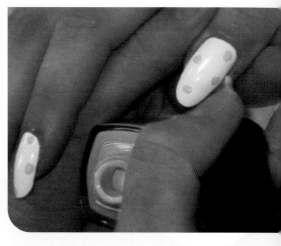

3 Add three or four dots of the first colour in a random pattern, using the side of the polish brush.

Shade suggestions

OPI Nail Lacquer in Alpine Snow
China Glaze Nail Polish in Shocking Pink
Color Club Nail Polish in Wham! Pow!
Barry M Nail Polish in Pure Turquoise
Orly Nail Polish in Fresh
Nails Supreme Black Nail Art Pen
Color Club Nail Polish in Almost Famous
Seche Vite Dry Fast Top Coat

5 Add random dots of a third colour, remembering to hold the hand steady.

6 Add a fourth colour to the nails in a dotted pattern.

7 If there's space on the nail, add a fifth and final colour, filling in any large white spaces on the nail.

8 Using a black nail art pen, create a random sequence of three lines around a dot of colour. Start with a straight line at the top and curve the other two, leaving a small space between each one.

4 Add another three or four dots of a second, contrasting bright colour.

Multi-coloured leopard print nails, designed on a white base shade to make the colours 'pop'.

9 Continue around all other dots of colour and add one or two dots or lines in any open white areas to prevent uniformity.

10 Repeat on the other nails and seal with a top coat.

Fashion fusion

In a step away from the classic red or French manicures that are worn to complement all fabrics, nail design is increasingly tailored around clothing collections, with experienced technicians creating both artistic and colour-complementary nails. Fashion houses are even embracing funky nail art to serve as the ultimate accessory to their clothing lines.

Nail art for fashion often allows for a lot of forward thinking and time for creation. Styles can range from block colours to highlight shades or detailed, intricate patterns to match a specific item. An ideal low-cost accessory, nail art can also serve as a tool to pull an outfit together or highlight an occasion, season or event. If bold, block colours are worn yet appear in need of some jazzing up, the shades can come together on the nail in a series of patterns or shapes to enliven the outfit and draw attention from the fabrics.

Above *Assorted black and white tribal-style nails by Sophie Harris-Greenslade.*

Left *Leopard-print nails with a feature fingernail by Christina Rinaldi.*

Above right *A bright step-style design with dotted detailing by Christina Rinaldi.*

Below *A stylish black manicure with random white and gold detailing by Christina Rinaldi.*

Left *A floral design by Sophie Harris-Greenslade, inspired by a Mary Katrantzou catwalk collection.*

Below *A multi-coloured design on false nails by Sophie Harris-Greenslade, inspired by a collection from Indian fashion designer Manish Arora.*

Left (from top) *Assorted designs on nail tips by Sophie Harris-Greenslade, inspired by a Manish Arora catwalk collection.*

Designs on nail tips by Sophie Harris-Greenslade, inspired by a collection by Meadham Kirchhoff.

Nail designs on plastic tips inspired by a collection by designer Peter Pilotto. Nails by Sophie Harris-Greenslade.

TECHNICIAN PROFILE
Ami Vega, USA

Travelling nail artist Ami Vega had her first brush with nail art at a young age, when she and a friend experimented with different polish colours on their nails. With an enthusiasm for art of all sorts, Ami started to elaborate on her nail décor and is now a highly sought-after nail artist in New York City. She seeks inspiration from pop art culture, bold patterns, textiles and fashion for her striking designs and chronicles her work and nail art journey on her website, El Salonsito.

Above *A kaleidoscope nail design featuring triangular shapes in five shades that complement the model's ring.*

Top right *A freehand paisley-print design across deep purple nails by Ami Vega.*

Centre right *A random mix of bright colours and designs including a crown, caricature and peace symbol.*

Above *A mixture of nail designs inspired by Keith Haring, an artist whose work was drawn from 1980s New York street culture.*

Left *Varying geometric designs across all fingertips featuring a neon yellow statement shade.*

Right *Bright, freehand designs featuring food and floral references.*

Below left *Squoval nails featuring a mixture of bright pink and glitter base shades with freehand detailing in a leopard-print style.*

Bottom left *Nude nails featuring a variety of bold colours and designs, suited to a wearer who may be indecisive or keen to experiment with nail styles and shades.*

Below *Neon multi-coloured nails with a leopard-print effect.*

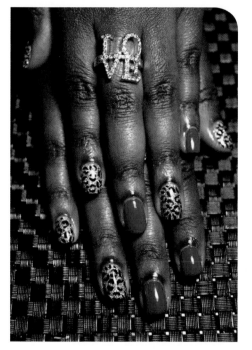

Tribal nails

Tribal nail designs combine geometric patterns and bright, contrasting colours. Dots, stripes and zigzag patterns are key, and the beauty of this style of nail art is that there is no limit as to the number of colours used on the nail. It is a popular choice for those with a little more time to spend, a steady hand and some degree of patience, as each colour must dry before painting around it to prevent smudging and colour bleeding. Experiment with base colour to complement fabrics and fashions.

PROJECT: TRIBAL NAILS By Ami Vega

1 Apply a base coat followed by two thin coats of a bright nail shade.

2 Create a 'V' shape in the middle of each nail using grey polish.

3 Fill in the space below the 'V' with a black nail striper and create another 'V' shape above the first one.

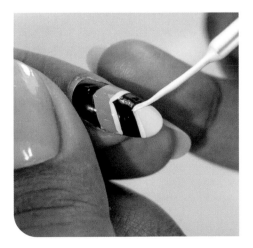

4 Outline the top black 'V' with a white striper and leave to dry.

5 Apply a top coat to seal the design and leave a glossy finish.

Shade suggestions

Pippa by Zoya
Alexandra's Hot Gray by Brucci
Q-Art nail art polish in white and black

A model shows oval nails with varied designs in just four shades, including a rope effect and striped tribal-style pattern.

Image gallery

Top left *A striking combination of half-moon manicure and French manicure styles with embellishment, by Ami Vega.*

Top right *Expressive nails with half-moon detailing by Ami Vega.*

Above *Nails inspired by UK fine artist and designer INSA and his graffiti background, by Ami Vega.*

Below *A mixture of texture and matte nails by Ami Vega.*

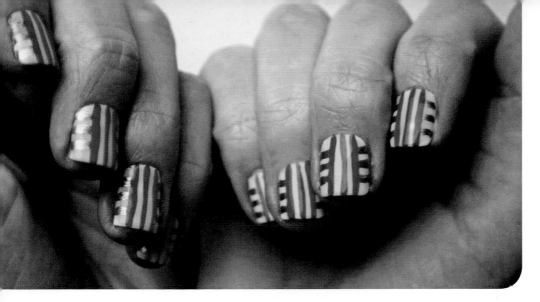

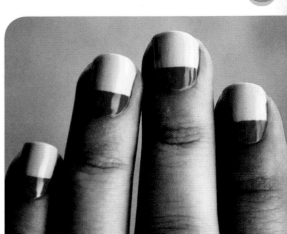

Above *Nude and orange nails with a straightened half-moon style by Christina Rinaldi.*

Above left *Nails with a coral and gold stripe effect by Christina Rinaldi.*

Left *Dusky beige nails with red block colour effects by Christina Rinaldi.*

Below left *A matchstick-inspired manicure by Christina Rinaldi.*

Below *A floral manicure with a gradient design on the statement nail by Christina Rinaldi.*

TECHNICIAN PROFILE
Christina Rinaldi, USA

Christina Rinaldi is a Brooklyn-based nail artist and creative designer. With unconventional methods of stencilling and colour mixing, every set of nails she produces is a study of technique and composition. Her background is in print and interactive design and she looks to culture and the runway to influence her precise nail designs. Christina has collaborated with leading beauty chain Sephora to create stylish sets of nail polish inspired by street fashion.

Above *A three-colour nail pattern with statement ring-finger designs.*

Right *Nails inspired by dripping paint.*

Below *Multi-coloured chevron-style nails.*

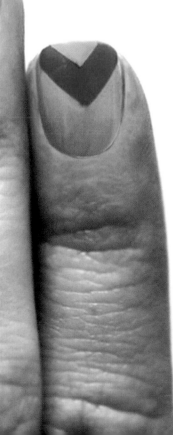

Above *Nails designed to create the illusion of small, sharp talons.*

Left *A crossover of block colour and neon dots.*

Below *An extension of the half-moon manicure with a dotted effect.*

Left *A floral manicure with a gradient design on the statement nail.*

PROJECT: CROSS-OVER POLKA DOT NAILS By Christina Rinaldi

Combine street style with popping colours and a twist on the half-moon manicure by creating a cross-over design that is quick to do but requires precision. Choose a dark shade as the main colour with a bright, contrasting shade for the dots for a quirky look.

1 After an application of base coat or a pale nude shade, apply your chosen colour in a diagonal line from the corner of the half-moon out towards the free edge. Apply two coats of polish to the upper half of the line and allow to dry.

2 Using a dotter and polish or striper in a contrasting colour, create a line of dots in the opposite direction from the other side of the half-moon towards its opposite free edge.

3 Using the first line of dots as a guide, apply further dots in a slightly angled direction upwards towards the free edge of the nail. Repeat on all nails and apply top coat when completely dry.

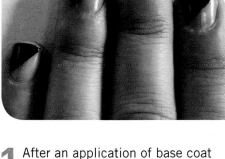

Shade suggestions

Ciaté Paint in Power Dressing
Orly Hotshot

Nude and teal nails with a contrasting neon dotted pattern give a simple yet striking effect.

CHAPTER FOUR:

ALL WRAPPED UP

The year of 2007 saw the arrival of Minx, a nail film that, when held under heat by a nail technician, is shrink-wrapped to fit either artificial or natural nails. Consumer versions of the concept slowly followed suit after the instant-effect foils, or 'wraps', proved a hit with both men and women as a fast and striking option for nail artistry.

Though they require some precision, nail foils are easy to apply and remove, need no drying time and come in numerous designs to suit all trends and occasions. Once in place, their longevity is about a week, and they are favoured by the time-poor and those who wish to make a statement with their nails by wearing a custom design or the latest patterns. They can also be cut and shaped to suit the nail or to play on past and present nail trends, such as the half-moon manicure. It's not hard to see why nail wraps have been revolutionary in convenient and intriguing nail design.

Left *Silver Nail Rock wraps featuring Swarovski crystal elements, designed and applied by Zoe Pocock.*

Wrap application

Zoe Pocock, creative director for Nail Rock, demonstrates how to apply nail wraps.

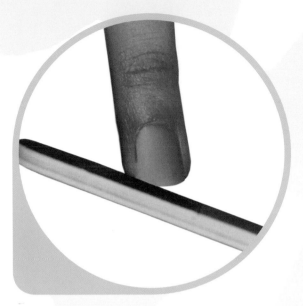

1 Push back the cuticle and shape and file the nail edge. Gently remove the surface shine with a nail buffer or smooth nail file.

2 Clean the nail with a sanitizer or nail preparation wipe. Select the wrap closest to the size of the cuticle (trim to fit if required) then warm the wrap between fingers or with the hot air from a hairdryer before removing from the backing sheet.

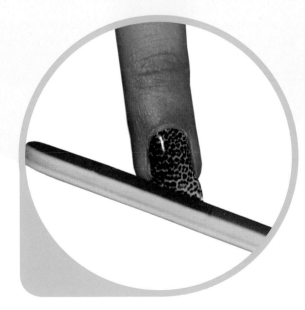

3 Place the wrap near the cuticle edge. Press firmly onto the nail and work from the cuticle edge, applying pressure and smoothing the wrap from the middle to the outside edges of the nail.

4 Smooth out any creases by lifting the wrap slightly and stretching back over the nail, before applying pressure and smoothing again. Extend the wrap over the free edge of the nail and file away the excess.

Below *Yellow cheetah print Nail Rock wraps, designed and applied by Zoe Pocock.*

Bottom *Gold giraffe print Nail Rock wraps, designed and applied by Zoe Pocock.*

Right *Quail-egg effect Nail Rock wraps, designed and applied by Zoe Pocock.*

TECHNICIAN PROFILE
Zoe Pocock, UK

Leading celebrity nail technician Zoe Pocock is the creative director for Nail Rock, the UK's leading nail wrap brand, which offers easy-to-apply designs inspired by trends. Zoe launches new Nail Rock designs seasonally and is no stranger to high-profile collaborations with fashion designers and lifestyle brands. Famed for creating iconic and innovative twists on the standard manicure, Zoe is a firm believer in nails as a fashion accessory and has teamed her work with top design houses Mulberry, Folli Follie, and Meadham Kirchhoff in New York.

Wrap stars & fashion shows

Extending fashion trends to fingernails, Minx and various other nail-wrap designs reflect seasonal looks and have featured in a number of high-end fashion shows and magazine shoots. Transforming the way the nail technician works, wraps can be custom-made in advance to suit the clothing collection, then applied and shaped in a matter of minutes.

A popular product with celebrities on account of their speedy application time, nail wraps also have a glossy or reflective finish which makes them an immediate focal point in photographs. Custom-made wraps can also feature faces and logos, with flag designs particularly favoured by patriots.

Above *Singer Rihanna wearing Minx nail foils featuring a print of Barack Obama, applied by Kimmie Kyees.*

Below *Beyoncé Knowles with gold hologram-style Minx foils, applied by Lisa Logan.*

Left *Rihanna with Black and Chrome Polka Dot Minx nail foils, applied by Kimmie Kyees.*

Above *Pop star Katy Perry wearing Minx in Silver Lightning, applied by Kimmie Kyees.*

Above right *Singer Eve wearing metallic snakeskin-style Minx nail foils, applied by Naja Rickette.*

Right *Pop star Ke$ha displaying Minx nail foils with additional embellishments, applied by Kimmie Kyees.*

Left *Singer Jordin Sparks wearing Golden Lightning Minx for a music video, applied by Kimmie Kyees.*

Below *Singer Fergie wearing black and silver striped Minx nail foils, applied by Naja Rickette.*

TECHNICIAN PROFILE
Naja Rickette, USA

Known as the 'Minx Master' for her inspirational work with the Minx brand of nail wraps, Naja occupies a variety of roles within the nail industry. She has her own range of Minx, which she designed herself, and co-hosts a weekly internet-based radio show, Nail Talk Radio, on which she shares her nail knowledge and offers business advice to fellow nail technicians. Naja also runs her own nail training academy and has a huge celebrity client base. Her custom nail art has appeared on magazine covers and in numerous music videos, editorial spreads, fashion shows and advertisements.

Naja's nail art designs are inspired by the client that she is working with; whether it be a couture nail, a ready-to-wear nail or just a simple accent nail, Naja believes that everyone should try nail art. Her signature style is to create nails that are all different but have a congruent theme. She attributes this to her previous career as a trained gourmet chef, where mixing a combination of ingredients that don't traditionally go together make a masterpiece.

Above *A translucent Minx nail foil layered over coloured nails, applied by Naja Rickette.*

Right *Minx nail foils in the transparent 'Johnny' design layered over the 'Lusion' style.*

Below *Naja wears tribal-style monochrome nail foils.*

Below right *Leopard print Minx nail foils on one hand, contrasting with silver and checkered Minx on the other hand.*

Opposite *A model wears a red and black nail design created using Minx nail foils to complement her lip shade.*

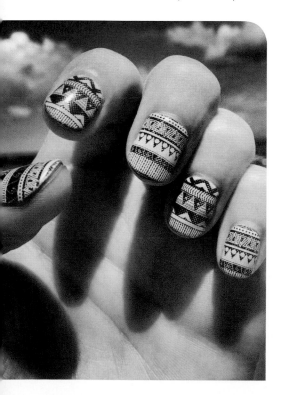

TECHNICIAN PROFILE
Lisa Logan, USA

Celebrity manicurist Lisa Logan has been offering high-end nail care to top entertainers since the mid-1990s, and her experience has made her one of the most sought-after nail-care experts within the industry. The hallmarks of Lisa's manicure and pedicure skills are the precision of her polish application, her custom-design nail art and her knowledge of overall nail care. Often travelling between New York and Los Angeles for high-profile bookings, Lisa is routinely called upon by top photographers and leading magazines for editorials and cover shoots. In 2008, Lisa began using Minx nails on her clients and has since designed her own lines of Minx. She has her own agency and salon and also acts as a consultant to a number of American beauty companies.

Top left *A model for design house Bess NYC wears Happy Dots Minx nail foils designed and applied by Lisa.*

Top right *Manicures featuring Minx nail foils custom-made for a catwalk show by design house Katie Ermilio.*

Above left *Custom-made Minx nail foils for a collection by designer Daniella Kallmeyer, applied by Lisa and the Nail Taxi team, USA.*

Left *A multi-coloured manicure featuring animal-print Minx nail foils, applied by Lisa for a Vogue Italy photo shoot.*

Image gallery

Above left *Monochrome Minx nail foils, applied by Leah Light.*

Above right *Checkered Minx nail wraps and contrasting statement nails, applied by Leah Light.*

Below left *A model wears a Minx nail design in green, applied by Lisa Logan.*

Below right *Minx nails in the colourful Barcode Maze design applied by Leah Light.*

TECHNICIAN PROFILE
Kimmie Kyees, USA

Freelance nail artist Kimmie Kyees has a wide range of credits, from A-list celebrities to high-profile events, fashion campaigns, editorials and music videos. Famed for her attention to detail, Kimmie has been a licensed nail professional since 1994 and has designed a line of professional nail wraps for Minx. She has been interviewed as a celebrity manicurist for a wide variety of magazine and online features and is known for providing a wide range of on-trend nail services.

Top *Custom-made Minx nail foils in a money design worn by singer Rihanna.*

Left *Singer Rihanna wearing Ruby Red Lightning Minx nail foils for a TV show.*

Above *Minx nail foils custom-made to feature the face of comedian Russell Brand, worn by singer Katy Perry.*

Right *Jordin Sparks wearing Minx foils customized with gold chains.*

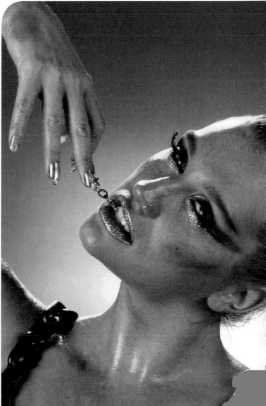

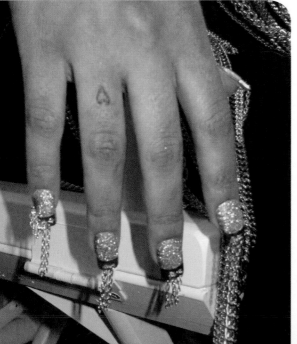

Above *Singer Ke$ha wearing custom-made nails featuring Minx nail foils for a video shoot.*

Above left *Rihanna wearing half-moon manicure Minx nail foils.*

Left *Custom-made bridal nails with 3D diamanté embellishment.*

CHAPTER FIVE:

FASHION-FORWARD FINGERTIPS

Runway nail styles in particular pave the way for mainstream nail-art trends and seasonal shades. While nude has been favoured as the 'fashion nail' for decades on account of its versatility, recent years have seen greater experimentation with style and form to produce nails that become part of a fashion collection's overall look.

Fashion designers set up meetings with hair stylists, make-up artists and nail technicians weeks in advance of a fashion show to discuss the looks that are required for the collection. Depending on the designer's view, the models' nails can be anything from one colour in a signature shade from the collection to long and sculpted, with or without nail decals, or in a print to complement the collection. Nail wraps can be custom-made in advance of the show to exactly replicate the fabric styles, and polish colours can be mixed or layered for exact shades.

While traditional nail polish is still prevalent backstage, the drying time means that it is susceptible to smudges by models and their dressers. Following the introduction of hybrid and gel polishes in 2010, which dry in under two minutes when cured under UV light, and under 20 seconds under LED light, many nail technicians have taken to using these instead. The service can be completed almost as quickly as traditional nail polish application and gel polishes have a similar colour range.

The abundance of materials that provide speedy effects on the nail has been a big factor in the nail-art boom on runways all over the world, as fashion-show preparation is on a tight schedule. There is not enough time backstage if the nail look requires fiddly decals or several stages of work, so a nail technician and his or her team will pre-produce the look on false nails or nail tips in their hundreds, then fit and shape them to each model's nail on the day of the show.

Nail fashion on runways can be as creative and as detailed as the designer wishes, and is now as important as the hair and make-up as designers recognize that the nails will be in photographs as much as the rest of the ensemble. Runway nail fashions are a piece of the collection that can be imitated at home to replicate the trend.

Left *Pale almond-shaped nails by Antonio Sacripante for Dsquared2.*

What makes a fashion nail?

PROFILE
Jan Arnold

Jan Arnold is the co-founder and style director of CND (formerly Creative Nail Design), a global leader in nail care and beauty. Often referred to as 'Fashion's first lady of nails', Jan is a key link between professional nail beauty and international high fashion and has pioneered custom nail styles for top designers all over the world.

'Nails are the ultimate fashion accessory – the perfect punctuation to an outfit and personality and a defining statement to style,' she says. *'With nails, there are 20 opportunities to thrill. In terms of nail colour and design trends, these develop on the runway and vary season by season. Since debuting at Fashion Week in 1996, CND has helped to make nails mainstream fashion accessories. Participating in Fashion Week has validated a place for nails, alongside the best in hair and make-up. Designers can now envisage the total look with the finishing touch of an interesting nail.*

'Nail style can be inspired by fabric design and texture, or a designer's muse when creating the collection. What's her personality, her whims, her alter ego? This reveals the attitude of the nails. Are they soft and sweet or sharp and femme fatale? Just as trends are culled from what is seen in fabrics, silhouettes and colours on the runway, trends emerge based on the nail look.

'In recent years, mainstream designers have become more open-minded to experimenting with colour, design and texture. Nail art is finally becoming mainstream because it is an easily obtainable runway statement. In the past few years, the widely acknowledged definition "nail art" has morphed from literal stars and rainbows to more sophisticated designs, which are now considered nail fashion.

'Nails are the ultimate fashion accessory – the power is in your hands!'

Left *A model for a Gareth Pugh collection sports a black-and-white nail look conceptualized by Marian Newman.*

Left *Short, rounded nails with a translucent pink overlay by Antonio Sacripante for Dsquared2. The nails are classic and well groomed, with just enough colour to complement the clothing without distracting the eye from the items in the collection.*

Below *Textured nails in a burgundy hue by Antonio Sacripante for a DSquared2 fashion show; complementing the make-up and the deep tones of the collection, the nail shade is warm and rustic, reflecting seasonal shades with added texture.*

TECHNICIAN PROFILE
Marian Newman, UK

Former forensic scientist Marian Newman has worked in almost every area of the nail industry. Her career began when she opened a salon in 1987, before progressing into training and consultative work for some of the largest nail companies in the UK.

Marian's expert knowledge has been called upon by the global print and broadcast media and she commands an unrivalled position in the field of session nail styling. She is one of the few top nail technicians whose work appears in glossy magazines around the world almost every week and her nail designs have been seen at fashion shows in London and Paris including Givenchy, Vivienne Westwood, Valentino, Moschino and McQueen. Marian has worked with some of the world's most legendary photographers, and career highlights include styling the nails for more than 50 *Vogue* covers and working on every advertising campaign for Christian Dior for over a decade.

Marian has also written *The Complete Nail Technician*, a definitive guide for budding nail practitioners, and launched an innovative nail colour and accessories range, alongside a series of designs in collaboration with the nail foil brand Minx.

Above left *Almond-pointed nails with a Minx overlay by Marian Newman for Gareth Pugh. The extrovert design complements the eye adornments and the toughness of the clothing, its colours serving to enhance the monochrome theme.*

Left *A model wears extended nails overlaid in black-and-white striped Minx for Gareth Pugh.*

Right *Nail wraps featuring variations on the half-moon manicure, applied by Marian for the Vivienne Westwood Red Label campaign.*

Opposite page *Chain mail nails created for Gareth Pugh.*

Nails as fashion

In an innovative and unique collaboration, nails have been seen as instrumental and influential in creating fashion designs. Controversial designer Charlie Le Mindu made history in 2011 when he presented his spring/summer 2012 collection in Paris with dresses and accessories made of more than 30,000 Minx nail coatings hand-wrapped over plastic nail tips. Marian Newman headed the team that created the nails and saw them come together as one with hair and make-up to make the fashion itself.

The photographs on this and the following spread show the foil-coated nails used for the clothes, head-dresses and models' fingernails. All the nail tips were coated in Minx nail foils by Marian Newman and her assisting nail team.

Top left *Close-up of a dress designed by Charlie Le Mindu made from nails covered in Minx foils.*

Opposite *Front and back views of a dress from the collection featuring hundreds of nail tips coated in Minx foils.*

Left *Spanish actress Rossy de Palma on the catwalk wearing an outfit made from nail tips covered in Minx foils.*

Above *A decorative headpiece for the show featuring nail tips wrapped in blue Minx nail foils.*

Left *A hooded viper headpiece for the collection made largely from plastic nail tips wrapped in blue and gold Minx foils.*

Above *A male model wears an intricate turban headpiece from the collection.*

Below *Models for the Charlie Le Mindu show wearing Minx nails.*

Above *A model wears a headpiece and underwear adorned with plastic nail tips wrapped in gold Minx. She also wears extended nails coated in Minx with a metallic tip.*

Right *Thousands of Minx nails were used to create this one piece with a plunging neckline for the collection.*

Below *Close up of a cobalt blue crew neck cap-sleeved dress on the runway.*

Left *A model sports fuchsia nails for a DSquared2 fashion show.*

TECHNICIAN PROFILE
Antonio Sacripante, Italy

Multi-lingual Antonio Sacripante travels all over the world to fulfil roles as a nail competition judge and trainer. A multi-award winner, he holds the title of 'Dean of Education' for one of the world's biggest nail brands and runs his own nail training academy in Italy alongside working with celebrities and for fashion channels. Antonio has headed up nail teams at various high-profile Fashion Week shows, including Dsquared2 and Les Copains at Milan Fashion Week, and encourages creative technicians to develop their skills and keep up with nail fashion trends through seminars and nail competitions.

Above *Pale, almond-shaped nails to complement a Dsquared2 collection.*

Right *Rounded, pale nails for a Dsquared2 show.*

Left *Deep burgundy textured nails were designed to complement the make-up for a Dsquared2 catwalk show.*

Left *Squoval nails with glitter effects for* Teen Vogue.

Below left *Nails in two shades of pink for an editorial campaign photographed by Marc Baptiste.*

Below *Almond-shaped red nails with a pink glitter half-moon effect for* Teen Vogue.

Opposite *Short blue, pink and green nails with blue glitter tips and effects for* Teen Vogue.

TECHNICIAN PROFILE
Myrdith Leon-McCormack, Haiti/USA

Born in Haiti, Myrdith emigrated to New York at a young age and developed a passion for the beauty industry. She has worked as a manicurist for leading celebrities and on advertising campaigns for some of the world's biggest brands, as well as for designers including Vera Wang, Carolina Herrera and Zac Posen. Passionate about her craft and a dedicated businesswoman, Myrdith launched her own line of nail products in 2008, M2M Natural Nail Care by damorejon.

Left *The multi-coloured 3D Caviar Manicure™ by Ciaté.*

CHAPTER SIX:

MAXIMIZING THE UNUSUAL

Rising social pressure for unique nails has led to increased experimentation with design, notably the products used. The opportunities are as endless as your imagination; nails can even be hung with feathers and chains to produce a colourful look with an unusual texture.

However good the adhesion, some unusual products used in nail artistry can last very little time and feel rough on the nail, so technicians often embed these materials within acrylic or gel products for a longer-lasting and smoother result. Small pieces of material, particularly lace, can look stylish on the nail or act as a stencil for nail design, and old pieces of jewellery or craft materials can help to create a unique nail look, tailored to suit a personality or ensemble.

Be Creative Blue Velveteen

Tweezers

Small scissors

Tool Kit: Unusual nail designs

What do you need?

1 Loose velvet in a desired shade for textured nails

2 Tweezers for the easy application of materials

3 Small scissors for cutting fabrics

4 An assortment of coloured polish shades, from dark to light and bright hues

5 A napkin or thin material with an interesting or seasonal print

6 A nail file for trimming and shaping

7 A cuticle pusher to smooth design materials

8 A clear top coat to seal the nail art

9 Gold leaf for unique and striking nails

Napkins

CND Marshmallow Rose

OPI My Private Jet

6

The Edge Nail Files

7

OPI Cuticle Stick

9

Gold Icaf

8

Seche Vite Top Coat

10 A strong base coat for long-lasting nail designs

11 Small, loose beads for textured nails

12 A sponge for use with polish and mesh

13 Mesh or tulle for a snakeskin nail effect

14 Nail Glue for easy adhesion of products

10

Orly Bonder

CND Stickey Base Coat

11

Small beads

TECHNICIAN PROFILE
Sam Biddle, UK

International nail judge and competition-winner Sam Biddle has found global success with her renowned design and colour skills. Since her first foray into the nail industry in 2000 she has produced front covers for magazines in Europe and the USA and has opened her own salon and nail academy, as well as starting Be Creative, a company that produces a series of nail-art tools and products. As an independent global educator, Sam teaches new and advanced skills to nail technicians and works with various distributors and product houses internationally, developing brands and providing training.

Left *Sculpted acrylic nails in a dripping paint design.*

Below left *Stiletto-shaped nail extensions featuring real snakeskin.*

Below *Pink ribbon-style nails created using the acrylic nail system.*

Right *Stiletto nails crafted from acrylic with real snakeskin encapsulated.*

PROJECT: SNAKESKIN EFFECT By Sam Biddle

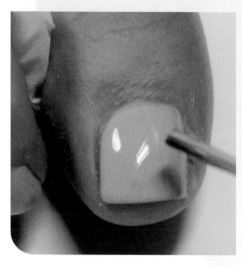

1 Prepare the nails by pushing back the cuticles and applying a good-quality base coat. Apply a nude polish in two thin coats, using one that is as close to the skin tone as possible. Alternatively, try a darker, bolder base colour.

2 Place a piece of tulle over the dry polish and hold firmly. For the tulle, try Original Sugar's Spun Sugar Kit, which also includes a sponge for applying colour.

3 Dab the sponge into a pink polish. Take off the excess polish and press the sponge down over the tulle onto the nail. You can dab all over or just on a section of the nail, depending on the look you want to achieve.

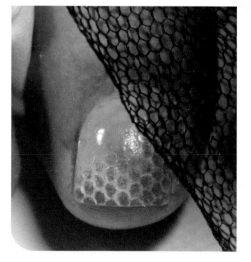

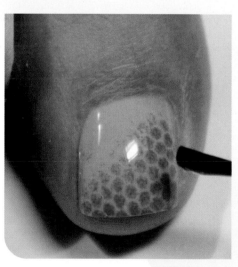

Shade suggestions

Orly Nail Polish in Sheer Peche
Orly Nail Polish in Hottie
Orly Polishield 3-in-1 Top Coat

4 Gently peel away the tulle to leave a snakeskin effect.

5 Apply a layer of top coat to the nails and allow to dry.

Nude nails with a pink snakeskin effect created using tulle and nail polish.

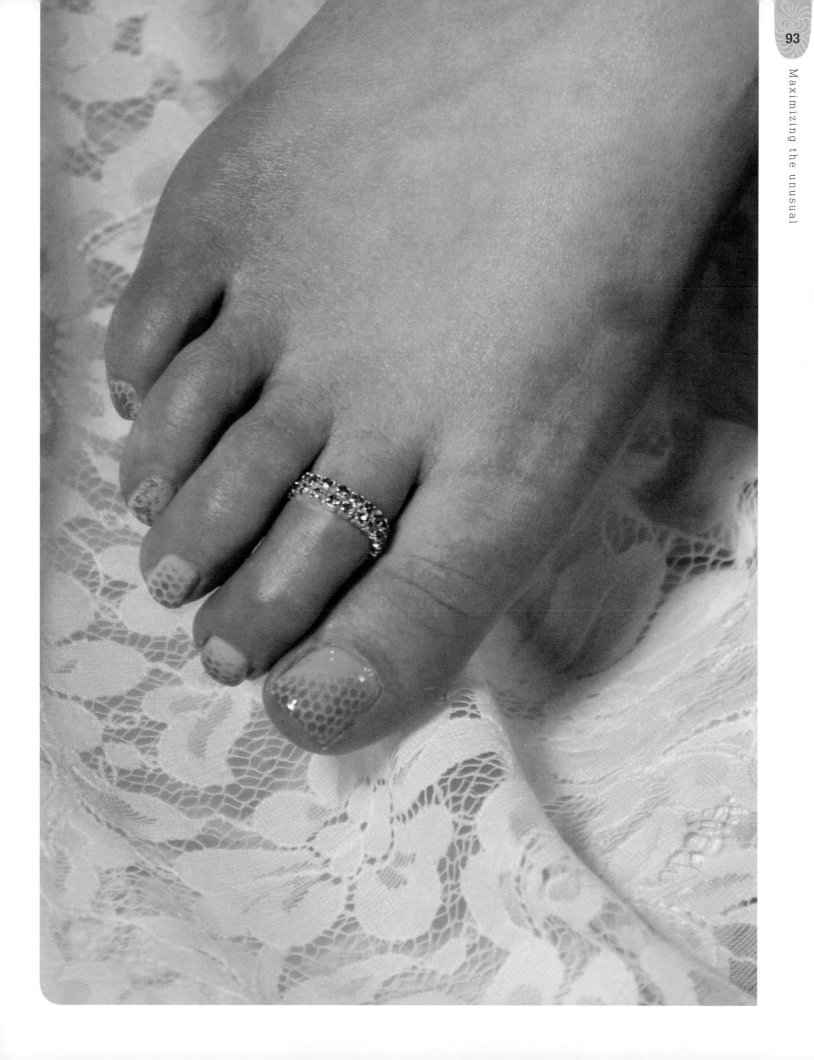

A touch of texture

Adding a new dimension to nails, the popularity of textured nail art has exploded with the increasing fascination with nail design. The 'Caviar Manicure', coined by UK nail brand Ciaté, features small beads sprinkled onto nail polish while wet for a colourful 3D effect. Closely following suit, the velvet manicure adds intrigue to a look with its furry look and feel and in an extension of the snakeskin effect, nail technicians have used real snakeskin in nail designs for a scaly appearance.

Above *Nails painted in bright shades and coated with corresponding colours of fine velvet pieces for a soft, textured nail effect, by Leah Light.*

Right *The dark blue 'Caviar Manicure', which leaves a 3D finish designed to replicate fish eggs, conceptualized by Charlotte Knight of nail brand Ciaté.*

Below *Mini models of trees painted pink and attached to false nails with wire, created by Megumi Mizuno.*

Bottom right *Pieces of lace cut from underwear and then encapsulated in acrylic nail extensions and finished with acrylic 3D detailing, by Erin Adeyemo.*

PROJECT: VELVET NAILS By Sam Biddle

1 Apply a base coat and two coats of your chosen nail polish.

2 While the polish is still tacky, apply gold leaf to the nail with tweezers. Seal with a top coat and allow to dry.

Nails painted in a purple shade before being dipped in purple velvet particles for a textured finish. These nails feature a statement design on the ring finger with the addition of gold leaf.

3 Apply a layer of top coat one nail at a time and dip into the bag of velvet particles. Gently press into the top coat while in the bag, then remove and leave for 30 seconds. Blow off the excess velvet.

Shade suggestions

Toma Nail Lacquer in It's a Girl Thing
Gold Leaf from Original Sugar
Purple Velveteen from Original Sugar

TECHNICIAN PROFILE
Denise Wright, UK

Salon owner, nail trainer, competitor and competition director Denise Wright has over 20 years of experience in the nail industry. An experienced beauty therapist and hairdresser, her passion and reputation lie in the nail sector and she holds multiple competition titles, including Nail Stylist of the Year. A globally respected judge, Denise assists at over 30 major nail competitions worldwide and educates on an international level, as well as testing and developing products for one of the largest nail companies in the world. Her knowledge of nail products and worldwide experience have been distilled in numerous trade magazines.

Top tip

Consider creating a French manicure style by polishing the nail in a chosen shade then applying a piece of napkin cut in the shape of a tip and sealing with a top coat.

Napkin nails make use of the printed patterns on napkins or serviettes to create quick and striking designs. Ideal for seasonal nails and those less at ease with freehand and intricate designs, the work involves cutting patterns from a napkin and incorporating them into nail work.

Top tips for Napkin Nail Art

1 Apply coloured polish after the base coat if desired to strengthen the design.

2 Always split the layers of the napkin and only apply the top layer with the design to the nail, as otherwise the paper is too thick for the top coat to seep through.

3 Apply an additional layer of top coat for a smooth finish.

4 If stick-on nails are to be used, complete the application of the napkin on these nails before affixing them to the natural nail.

5 Press the napkin firmly onto the nail for around 20 seconds or until it moulds to the nail plate.

PROJECT: NAPKIN NAILS By Denise Wright

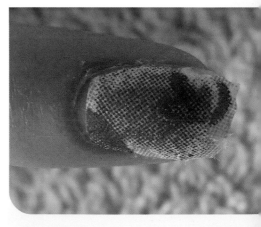

1 While the base coat is drying, cut the napkin to approximately the right size to fit the nail. Do not apply at this stage.

2 Trim the napkin neatly around the cuticle and sidewalls but keep the length.

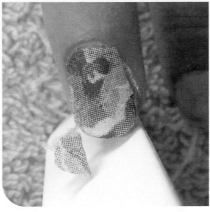

3 Apply a top coat directly over the base coat. While it is still wet, place the napkin piece onto the top coat and hold onto the nail. Use tweezers if required. The top coat will seep through the napkin, forming a seal.

4 While the top coat is still wet, apply another layer over the top of the napkin design.

5 When dry, cut and file the excess napkin until the free edge of the nail is met.

6 Repeat on all nails and seal the free edge with top coat or nail glue to prevent the napkin from peeling.

Nails with a floral finish created by sandwiching cuttings from a napkin between a base and top coat.

CHAPTER SEVEN:

INTRICATE NAIL DESIGNS

Using thoughtful colour combinations with skill, technique and imagination can produce nail art that stuns with its intricacy and detail. Nail technicians with artistic flair can employ professional products such as acrylic or gel to sculpt long nails in a variety of colours and with different effects, often embedding nail art materials within their designs.

Suited to delicate hands on account of the often extended shape and pointed tip, nail art of this form can be completely customized and often takes hours to produce. The craftsmanship requires precision and patience, and technicians seek inspiration from all around for their designs.

Mixing a variety of nail art mediums can produce exquisite results such as figurines and 3D detailing which are often shown off at competitions in a test of skills in handling products and tools. At the beginning of the 21st century, technicians turned to the art world and found inspiration for the one-stroke nail-art technique. It is especially popular for painting flowers on the nail, as the artist blends, shades and highlights using a variety of brushes to create a particularly detailed image.

Left *Sweetcorn-style nails sculpted using the acrylic nail system, crafted by Kirsty Evita Meakin.*

TECHNICIAN PROFILE
Kirsty Evita Meakin, UK

Kirsty Evita Meakin is recognized as one of the best nail artists in the world. A regular presence at global nail competitions, she has over 50 nail accolades, including the titles of Nail Artist of the Year and UK Nail Professional of the Year 2010. Kirsty has been honing her nail skills for over 15 years after uncovering her creative prowess at a Youth Training Scheme. The advancement of nail products has allowed Kirsty to explore her ability and passion for nail art and she is mainly recognized for her freehand and 3D skills.

A regular judge at both national and international nail competitions and a speaker at various nail forums, Kirsty is passionate about the education of promising nail technicians and has helped to develop a new concept for learning nails skills online.

Below *Nails sculpted as mini sweetcorn pieces, using the acrylic nail system.*

Below right *Sculpted angular nails with a black tip and white dotted effect.*

Right *Stiletto-shaped enhancements with a hand-painted pink and white bow effect.*

Opposite *Rock chick-style enhanced nails with colour gradient and black detailing.*

Style, shape and form

Artificial nail sculpture gives a technician freedom to design a shape, length or style to suit both the wearer's nail and the design idea. Stiletto shapes, where the nail is sculpted into a lengthy point, ooze femininity and allow for the design to be concentrated in the extended nail tip.

Historically, long nails have been associated with elevated social status, since the wearer could not be someone who was engaged in manual labour. The Ancient Egyptians wore artificial nails created from ivory, gold or bone to make their fingertips look as expensive as possible, and China's Chou Dynasty saw people of a high status grow long nails to indicate their status, with the colour of their nails serving to reveal their social class. Persons of lower social ranking wore black and red shades on their nails to represent strength, while the gold and silver shades worn by the elite indicated power and a high rank.

Longer nails in the present day are largely grown just for decoration, and artificial lengthening has come a long way since the Ancient Egyptians used natural and often valuable materials. Nails sculpted with acrylic have grown in popularity since 1957, when Dr Frederick A. Slack Jr, a leader in prosthetic dentistry, used dental acrylic and aluminium foil to fix his cut thumbnail. From here, colours and techniques developed from dental products gave technicians the ability to produce elongated nails that could be embellished with imaginative and artistic additions.

Above *Acrylic stiletto nails with gold bubble detailing by Marta Lupka.*

Below *Enhanced nails featuring hand-painted hearts and swirls by Iryna Giblett.*

The practice of sculpting has led to innovations in the shape of enhanced nails. Angular designs such as the 'lipstick nail', crafted with the tip shaped to reflect that of a lipstick, are striking, while a skilled practitioner can create 3D additions for the top of the nail. However, acrylic and gel are also used to simply enhance the natural nail shape or redefine its contours before adding nail art.

Opposite top *Glitter gradient acrylic stiletto nails featuring diamanté embellishments by Marta Lupka.*

Opposite left *Blue mix sculpted acrylic nails with a rounded tip and silver and black hand-painted detailing by Lulú Desfassiaux.*

Opposite right *Stiletto acrylic nails with Grecian-themed hand-painted designs and diamanté embellishments by Lulú Desfassiaux.*

TECHNICIAN PROFILE
Lulú Desfassiaux, Mexico

A former lawyer, Lulú has been working with nails since the early 1990s and is a regular participant in international training events and competitions. As a multi-award winner, holding champion titles in mixed media and fantasy nail art competitions, she is recognized as a Global International Master Artist. Lulú's real passion lies in training fellow professionals to a global standard and she has developed her own international acrylic nail brand suited to lovers of nail art, colour and 3D techniques.

Left *An extended alternative to the French manicure style, featuring a hand-painted floral design and embellishments.*

Below left *Sculpted nails with a turquoise stiletto tip and hand-painted detailing.*

Below *Floral sculpted nails featuring hand-painted detailing and embellishments.*

Opposite *Romance-themed acrylic nails with hand-painted detailing and gold-leaf additions.*

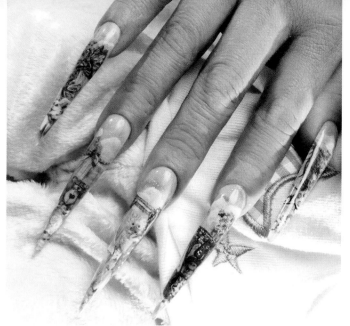

Above *Square sculpted nails with a hand-painted design inspired by ceramics.*

Above right *Stiletto nails with hand-painted cartoon animal designs.*

Left *Bamboo-inspired nails, featuring glitter encapsulated in an acrylic stiletto shape with black-and-white hand-painted detailing.*

Right *Sculpted acrylic nails with a rounded tip featuring hand-painted designs on the theme of the animated film* Cars.

Below *Multi-coloured acrylic powders and glitters encapsulated within an acrylic stiletto nail and finished with black hand-painted detailing.*

Right *Acrylic stiletto nails with lace encapsulated and hand-painted floral designs.*

Opposite left *A glittery stiletto design featuring 3D floral additions.*

Opposite right *Black stiletto nails sculpted with acrylic with 3D gold glitter sculpted embellishments.*

Opposite bottom *Gold and black gradient nails with red diamanté embellishments.*

TECHNICIAN PROFILE
Marta Lupka, Poland

Marta's creative tendencies became evident at a young age, when she began to create her own artworks in drawing and painting. Her adventure with nail design began in 2009, and her highly acclaimed perfectionism has led to a Nail Artist of the Year title and a role as a master educator for a UK nail brand. Marta's signature style, a long stiletto nail shape, is achieved using acrylic. Inspired by art, her work presents ideal shapes and proportions and all nail designs are precisely planned and sketched on paper before creation.

Left *A gold and green stiletto acrylic nail design.*

Below *Stiletto nails with gold and effects crafted using acrylic.*

Right *Purple and gold stiletto nails with an acrylic honeycomb effect.*

Below right *Galaxy-themed acrylic stiletto design with gold acrylic 3D detailing.*

Far right *A purple gradient acrylic design with hand-painted floral detailing.*

Mixing media and skillsets

To show the extent of a technician's skill with nail art products and materials, competitions for mixed media nail art are held globally. Competitors push their abilities to the max to complete a design across nail tips, generally consisting of a mixture of hand-painted nail art designs, 3D nail art and sculptured nails. A theme must be followed on all five nails to showcase how far imagination can stretch. Similarly, there are competitions for hand-painted nail art that follow a theme and are designed to test a technician's attention to detail and artistic flair in a specified timeframe.

From top left *A wintry design on nail tips using various nail skills and materials by Kirsty Evita Meakin.*

A vampire-themed scene across ten nail tips using a variety of nail art materials, by Iryna Giblett.

A hand-painted graffiti style scene on nail tips by Kirsty Evita Meakin.

Left *A woodland fairy design on nail tips by Kirsty Evita Meakin.*

Above *A hand-painted urban graffiti-inspired design by Kirsty Evita Meakin.*

Above *Stiletto acrylic nails with a sculpted floral design by Lulú Desfassiaux.*

Above right *Hand-painted nail tips by Lulú Desfassiaux with sculpted acrylic 3D detailing to honour the animated film* Hop.

Below *A design across ten nail tips inspired by sea creatures, featuring hand-painted and 3D sculpted designs and embellishments, by Lulú Desfassiaux.*

Right *A mythical creatures design across ten nail tips with acrylic detailing, embellishments and hand-painted effects, by Lulú Desfassiaux.*

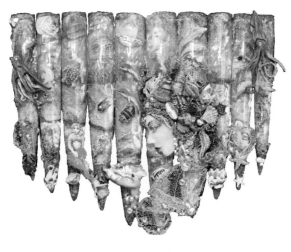

TECHNICIAN PROFILE
Virginia Arleo, Argentina

Virginia Arleo began her nail career in her mother's salon in Argentina. On a trip to the US, she saw the work of two of her nail idols, Tom Holcomb and Danny Haile, which furthered her passion for the craft. Specializing in intricate and artistic designs, Virginia is a frequent participant in nail competitions and has won multiple titles all over the world. She is classed as one of the world's 25 greatest nail competitors and is an educator and representative for one of the biggest global manufacturers of beauty products.

Left *Here 3D theatrical designs are sculpted using acrylic on nail tips.*

Below *A mythical and Asian-inspired design with 3D sculpted embellishments and beading.*

Bottom left *Female characters depicted on nail tips sculpted from acrylic, with hand-painted detailing.*

Bottom right *Pink and black sculpted stiletto nails.*

Above Squoval-shaped acrylic nails with 3D acrylic designs and embellishments.

Left Nails with a festive theme, featuring acrylic embellishments and hand-painted details.

TECHNICIAN PROFILE
Iryna Giblett, Ukraine

Originally a microbiologist, Iryna discovered her passion for nail enhancements and nail art in 1998. She qualified as a nail technician during the same year, and since moving to Sweden in 2006, she has developed an international reputation as a nail artist, magazine editor, competitor, educator and competition judge. Her work has been published in professional nail magazines worldwide and she has established the first school in Scandinavia to specialize in advanced nail art education. Aside from stunning nail art creations, Iryna has her own range of professional nail products and enjoys educating and inspiring other nail technicians.

CHAPTER EIGHT:

FANTASY FINGERNAILS

Impractical and wacky but astoundingly technical, fantasy nail art tends to be crafted only by patient and highly skilled nail technicians for competition purposes. The elaborate 3D art is usually based around a theme and employs professional nail products to craft and sculpt intricate figurines that are then applied to the nail and enhanced by a model's costume.

Often taking months of hard work and pushing product and skill to the limit, fantasy nail art can also involve interactive and moving parts as well as an abundance of colour and add-ons such as fairy lights and spinning wheels. While nail art such as this is not intended for everyday wear, themes can be replicated in a very basic form to suit a more practical, wearable style, using ready-made appliqués to make a nail really stand out.

Left *Firework-themed nails by Sam Biddle.*

Left *Fantasy nail art with a Kentucky Derby theme created for a competition in Orlando. The design features rosettes, horses and their riders, and when the fingers are held together, the nail art becomes a bouquet of flowers.*

Opposite *Mythology-themed fantasy nail art by Catherine Wong for a competition in Las Vegas. The designs feature dragons, Greek legends and religious figures.*

TECHNICIAN PROFILE
Catherine Wong, Singapore

Catherine Wong is a highly respected contributor to the nail industry as an international educator, judge, active competitor and product development advisor for manufacturers. Her work has been featured in numerous international nail publications and she is a prominent guest artist in the USA, Europe, Mexico, Australia, Korea, Japan and Asia. She has won numerous Nail Artist of the Year awards and her role in education for the nail industry is highly respected, particularly in Singapore and Malaysia.

Catherine Wong's five top tips for re-creating fantasy nail art

1 Think outside of the box; the more unusual the design, the more effective it will be.

2 Set aside a good deal of time to work on your nail creations.

3 Be imaginative and dedicate yourself to the cause; brainstorm ideas on paper before creating in 3D.

4 Think carefully about the story you want to tell on your nail and experiment with style and colour to reflect this.

5 Take application and creation at a slow and steady pace, concentrating on one nail at a time.

Far Left *Art deco inspired nails crafted to the theme of 'Roaring 20's'. Catherine was awarded first place for her design at a competition in Orlando.*

Left *Nails with a psychedelic 60's theme. The nails feature prints and colours iconic of the era, as well as peace signs and retro clothing.*

Left *Nails crafted with a dog show theme for a fantasy nail art veteran competition in Orlando. The nails were awarded first prize and feature vintage-style pin-up models and a variety of dog breeds to help tell a story.*

Above *Fantasy nails inspired by Cirque Du Soleil, featuring masks and sculpted acrobat figures.*

Fantasy image gallery

Above *A sculpted angel and a devilish character depict an angels and devils theme in a fantasy nail art concept by Cristóbal Cervera Barques.*

Below *Fantasy nail art by Cristóbal Cervera Barques on the theme of the seven deadly sins.*

Right *Iryna Giblett sculpts sea-themed designs on nail tips; featuring mermaids, fish and pirates.*

Below right *Mythical figures by Cristóbal Cervera Barques.*

Left *Woodland and mythical creatures sculpted by Lulú Desfassiaux for a fantasy nail art competition in London.*

Below *A goblin sculpted with acrylic for a fantasy nail design by Lulú Desfassiaux.*

Bottom left *Fairies, goblins and toadstools feature on fantasy nails by Lulú Desfassiaux.*

Bottom right *Sculpted mythical creatures, such as dragons and fairies, make up some of the fantasy nails by Lulú Desfassiaux.*

TECHNICIAN PROFILE
Viv Simmonds, Australia

With over 20 years experience in the nail industry, Viv Simmonds has achieved international recognition through her accomplishments, which include winning numerous nail competitions and gaining the title of Australian Champion for four consecutive years. Viv has judged nail competitions internationally and created front covers for a number of leading nail magazines, as well as featuring on television and in consumer magazines. A mentor of multi-award-winning nail artists, Viv travels all over the world to conduct unique training events in advanced nail technology and design.

Above left *Canine nail designs for a 'Dog Show' fantasy nails competition theme.*

Left *Here fantasy nails have a Spanish theme, including bull fighting and flamenco.*

Above *3D nail art on tips crafted for a competition theme entitled 'Everything Big in Texas'.*

Right *A flamenco dancer and fan appear in Viv Simmonds' fantasy nails design for a nail competition held in Singapore.*

Below *These fantasy nails were created for a competition with the theme 'It's all Greek to Me'.*

Picture credits & acknowledgements

Front cover © Kirsty Meakin
Title page © Christina Rinaldi
Half title page © Lulú Desfassiaux
4L © Lulú Desfassiaux, **4C** © Ami Vega; **6** © John Springer Collection/CORBIS;
7 © Leah Light

Chapter 1
8–9 © Lena White Ltd/OPI UK; **10** © Condé Nast Archive/CORBIS; **15L** © Kimmie
Kyees; **15C** © Christina Rinaldi; **15R** © Ami Vega; **17** © Gerrard International/
Jessica UK; **18, 19BL, 19BR** © Bio Sculpture Gel UK; **19T** © Megumi Mizuno;
20–21 © Leighton Denny Expert Nails

Chapter 2
22 © Nazila Love Glamour; **26** © Supa Nails; **28, 29TL, 29B, 30–31, 32B, 33,
34, 35** © Leah Light; **29TR** © NSI UK; **32T** © Megumi Mizuno; **36–37** © Lena
White Ltd/OPI UK

Chapter 3
38, 50–51, 54 © Ami Vega; **41–45, 48TL, 49TR, 49BR, 49L** © Sophie Harris-
Greenslade/The Illustrated Nail; **43TL, 46–47** © Helena Biggs; **48L, 48B, 49TL,
55-59** © Christina Rinaldi; **52–53** © Emil Baez

Chapter 4
60, 62, 63 © Rock Cosmetics/Nail Rock; **64TL, 64BC, 64BR, 65T, 65B, 70BL,
70TR, 71** © Kimmie Kyees; **64BL, 70BR** © Adam Orchon; **65R** © Meeno; **65CR,
67TL, 67BL** © Naja Rickette; **66** © Tiffany Kyees; **67TR** © Brandon Showers;
67BR © www.vitaljuice.com; **68TL** © Joseph Richards; **68TR** © Kate Ermilio;
68CL © Becky Yee; **68BL** © Lisa Logan; **69** © Leah Light; **70TL** © Tiffany Kyees

Chapter 5
72, 75, 82–83 © Max Salani Fotografo (www.maxsalani.it); **74, 76, 78–81** ©
Becky Maynes; **77** © CND (Creative Nail Design Inc.); **84T, 84BR, 85** © Vital
Agibalow for Teen Vogue; **84BL** © Marc Baptiste for Cosmopolitan magazine
USA, 2010

Chapter 6
86, 94R © Ciaté; **90L, 90BR** © Stuart Dibbon; **90BL, 91** © Paul de Villeneuve;
92–93, 95 © Sam Biddle; **94TL** © Leah Light; **94BL** © Tomohiro Muramatsu;
94BR © Erin Adeyemo; **96–97** © Denise Wright

Chapter 7
98, 100BL, 101 © Cameo Modern; **100TR, 100BR, 112T, 112B, 112R** © Kirsty
Evita Meakin; **102T, 103T, 108–111** © Marta Lupka; **102B, 112CTR, 115** ©
Bob Giblett, Iryna Giblett Nail Academy; **103BL, 103BR, 104–107, 113** © Lulú
Desfassiaux; **114** © Virginia Arleo